The True Story of

THE SALEM WITCH HUNTS

Amelie von Zumbusch

PowerKiDS
press.

New York

For Yvonne, Meryl, and everyone else who put up with my Salem-imposed gloominess

Published in 2009 by The Rosen Publishing Group, Inc.
29 East 21st Street, New York, NY 10010

First Edition

Editor: Nicole Pristash
Book Design: Kate Laczynski
Photo Researcher: Jessica Gerweck

Photo Credits: Cover, p. 1 © Age Fotostock.com; pp. 5, 9, 13, 15, 19, 21 © North Wind/North Wind Picture Archives; pp. 7, 17 © Getty Images, Inc.; p. 11 © Superstock.com.

Library of Congress Cataloging-in-Publication Data

Zumbusch, Amelie von.
  The true story of the Salem witch hunts / Amelie von Zumbusch. — 1st ed.
      p. cm. — (What really happened?)
  Includes index.
  ISBN 978-1-4042-4479-5 (library binding)
  1. Witchcraft—Massachusetts—Salem—History. 2. Trials (Witchcraft)—Massachusetts—Salem—History.
I. Title.
  BF1576.Z86 2009
  133.4'3097445—dc22
                                                  2008002085

Manufactured in the United States of America

CONTENTS

WHAT WERE THE SALEM WITCH HUNTS?

In 1692, a witch hunt started in Salem Village, Massachusetts, and spread to several nearby towns. Hundreds of people were **accused** of witchcraft and 20 were killed for being witches. However, **historians** now know that these people were not witches at all. The Salem witch hunts were very frightening because some people were treated so horribly by others.

When people think of the Salem witch hunts, many picture scary women in pointed black hats or mean witches from scary stories. However, let's take a look at the true story and learn what really happened in this small town.

Here an older woman is being accused of witchcraft and taken for questioning by Salem villagers. People of all ages and backgrounds were accused.

PURITAN MASSACHUSETTS

The Salem witch hunts took place in eastern Massachusetts. In the 1600s, a group of English people called the Puritans settled there. The Puritans wanted to practice their own form of **Christianity**. They were badly treated in England, so they came to Massachusetts to live as they wished.

Puritans were stricter, or firmer, than other Christians. They valued hard work and disliked fancy, or very nice, clothes. For the Puritans, all things were either good and from God or evil and tied to the Devil. Puritans feared and believed in witches. They thought witches were people who worked with the Devil.

Puritans generally wore plain, black and white clothing. They lived very simple lives, and they valued their faith and hard work.

THE TROUBLES BEGIN

In 1689, a Puritan **minister** named Samuel Parris moved to Salem Village with his family. Salem Village was a small settlement northwest of the town of Salem. Parris also brought two **slaves**, Tituba and John Indian, who likely came from Barbados.

Since most slaves in American history were African-American, people often think Samuel Parris's slaves were, too. However, historians believe Tituba and John Indian were Native Americans from Barbados.

Though Samuel Parris was drawn into some disagreements among the villagers, the Parrises lived peacefully until January 1692. Then, Parris's 9-year-old daughter, Elizabeth, and his 11-year-old niece, Abigail Williams, started having fits. The girls moved wildly and said things nobody could understand. Worst of all, the girls could not explain why they were doing these things!

This picture shows what the fits of Elizabeth Parris and Abigail Williams may have looked like. The fits scared the people of Salem, and they didn't know how to stop them.

ARE THESE GIRLS BEWITCHED?

Parris asked a doctor to look at the girls. The doctor suggested they were bewitched, or under a witch's power. A villager suggested they make a witch cake out of **rye** and the girls' **urine**, and then feed it to a dog. This was said to be a test for witchcraft. Tituba made the witch cake, but when Samuel Parris found out, he was angry. Parris thought that making a witch cake was like "going to the Devil for help against the Devil."

That February, the girls' fits grew even worse. Other village girls, such as Ann Putnam, began having fits as well.

Dunking, shown here, was another test for witchcraft. Puritans believed if a woman floated in the water, she was a witch. If she sank, or dropped, she was not a witch.

11

THE FIRST CONFESSION

The villagers asked the girls who was bewitching them. After some time, they named Tituba. Parris beat Tituba to try to get her to confess, or own up, to being a witch. However, Tituba said she was **innocent**. The girls accused villagers Sarah Good and Sarah Osborne of being witches, too.

Sarah Good and Sarah Osborne did not often go to church. Good was poor, and Osborne was angry and old. This made it easier for the villagers to believe they were witches.

On March 1, 1692, Tituba, Good, and Osborne were questioned. Some people even tried to trick the women into confessing. Then, Tituba confessed out of fear. She said that Osborne and Good were also witches. Tituba said they served the Devil and rode on a stick to visit the girls and hurt them.

Many villagers, like the man shown here, were scared of Tituba. Tituba was a slave, so it was easy for the villagers to look down on her.

13

MORE PEOPLE ARE ACCUSED

Tituba, Good, and Osborne were put in **jail**, but the matter did not end there. On March 11, Ann Putnam claimed Martha Corey was a witch and that Corey's **specter** was hurting her. Corey was a church member, so the villagers were surprised she was accused.

A week later, Abigail Williams named Rebecca Nurse, a woman known for her goodness, as a witch.

By April, Nurse, Corey, and Sarah Good's four-year-old daughter, Dorcas, were all jailed for witchcraft. Soon, many more were accused. Many people, like John Proctor, who suggested some of the accused were innocent, were accused themselves.

Many people think of witches as women. However, some of the accused were men, such as John Proctor, George Burroughs, and George Jacobs.

This painting shows Martha Corey being questioned about witchcraft. Some people believe the girls accused Corey only because she had called the girls liars.

15

FAMILIES ACCUSE

On June 2, 1692, Bridget Bishop was hanged for being a witch. Though Bishop was not among the first people charged with witchcraft, she was brought to **trial** first. Many knew she would be found **guilty**. Bishop's husband even claimed she was a witch!

The accusations of witchcraft soon spread beyond Salem Village. People in the nearby towns of Andover, Salem, Beverly, and Topsfield were accused of witchcraft, too.

Many people on trial for witchcraft had been accused by their own family members. Family members often turned on each other. They noticed that those who had confessed to witchcraft and accused others were not being brought to trial. Many family members were scared, and they lied to save themselves.

The witch trials, like the one shown here, often got out of hand. The young accusers would often scream and yell in fits, just like the fits that caused the accusations.

17

A HORRIBLE TIME

In the following months, eighteen people were hanged for witchcraft. Five others died in jail. One man who refused to stand trial was killed by having heavy rocks pressed on his chest. Like Bridget Bishop, these people were all innocent. They were killed because they would not confess to something of which they were not guilty.

In time, people started doubting the accusations. The girls started naming even more powerful people. Increase Mather, a powerful minister, questioned if stories about being hurt by specters should even be used in trials. People were then found innocent. In May 1693, the governor forgave everyone still jailed for witchcraft.

Samuel Sewell (right) was one of the judges during the Salem witch trials. After the trials were over, Sewell told the villagers he was sorry for the part he played.

A REASON FOR THE WITCH HUNT

Though the Salem witch hunt died out in 1693, it had been a long, horrible nightmare. Today, many people think the girls who accused others of witchcraft suffered from hysteria. This means they acted in ways they could not control or understand. The girls may have acted that way to go against the strict, hard way the Puritans treated girls.

Others think Tituba taught the girls a type of magic, called voodoo. They think the girls got scared of what Tituba showed them. Then, the girls accused Tituba to keep themselves out of trouble because the girls knew their parents would be angry.

Here Tituba is telling the young girls scary stories. Some people think that these dark stories were the cause of the girls' fits.

WHAT REALLY HAPPENED?

Some historians think disagreements in Salem Village caused the witch hunt. Many of the people who were accused of witchcraft once disagreed with the powerful Putnam family. Some believe the family made Ann Putnam and the girls accuse their enemies to get rid of them. The possible causes for the accusations go on and on, but we may never know the truth.

In 1706, Ann Putnam said she was sorry for what she had done 16 years earlier. Putnam said that at that time, she thought she had been under the power of the Devil.

Were the girls under the power of the Devil? Were they scared of getting in trouble? Did the Putnam family make them do it? Though we may never know the reason, we must make sure witch hunts like these never happen again.

GLOSSARY

accused (uh-KYOOZD) Said to have done something bad.

Christianity (kris-chee-A-nih-tee) A faith based on the teachings of Jesus Christ and the Bible.

guilty (GIL-tee) Having done something wrong or against the law.

historians (hih-STOR-ee-unz) People who study the past.

innocent (IH-nuh-sent) Doing no wrong.

jail (JAYL) A building where people who do a crime are locked up.

minister (MIH-nuh-ster) A person who leads services in a church.

rye (RY) A grass plant that people and animals eat.

slaves (SLAYVZ) People who are owned by other people and forced to work for them.

specter (SPEK-ter) Something the Puritans believed in that looked like a witch and was sent by that witch to hurt people.

trial (TRYL) When a case is decided in court.

urine (YUR-un) A waste made by the body.

INDEX

WEB SITES

Due to the changing nature of Internet links, PowerKids Press has developed an online list of Web sites related to the subject of this book. This site is updated regularly. Please use this link to access the list:
www.powerkidslinks.com/wrh/salem/